ANIMAL BATTLES

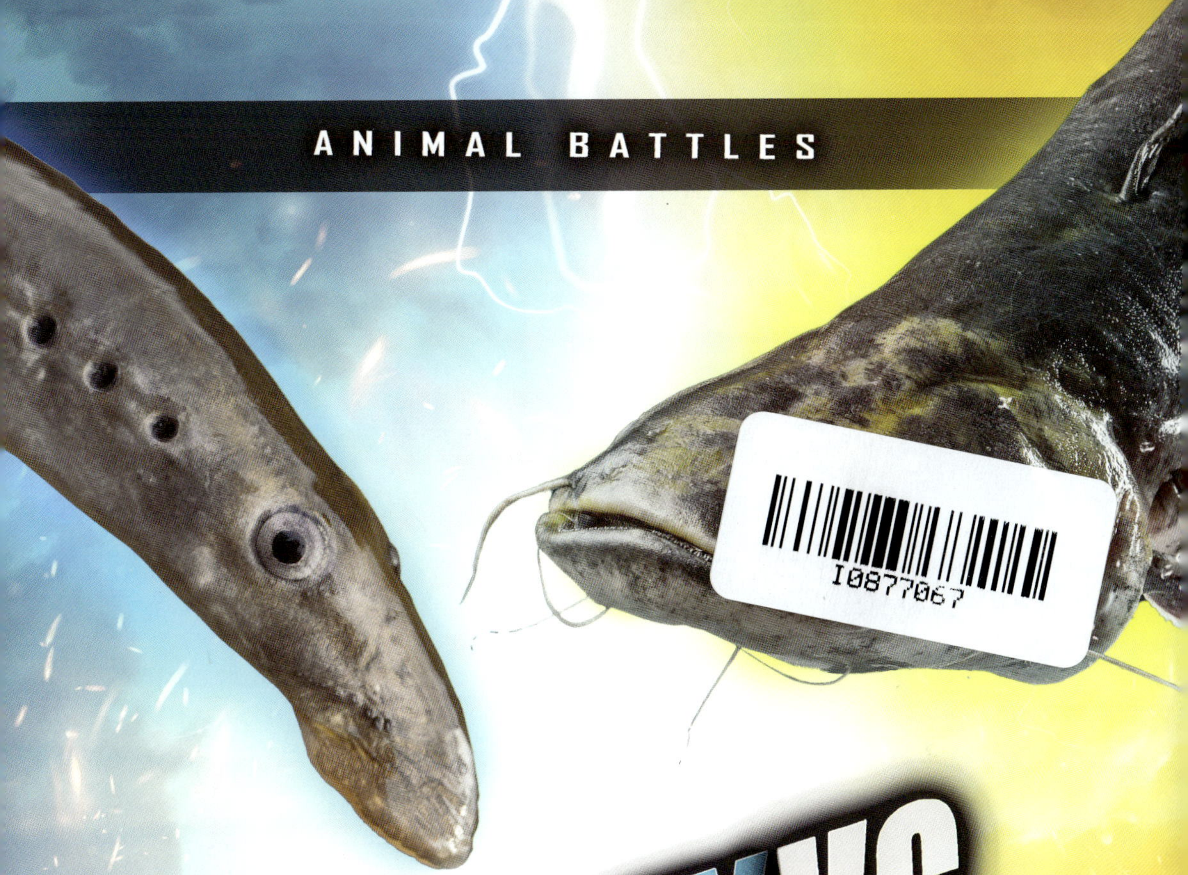

LAMPREY VS. CATFISH

BY NATHAN SOMMER

TORQUE™

Torque brims with excitement perfect for thrill-seekers of all kinds. Discover daring survival skills, explore uncharted worlds, and marvel at mighty engines and extreme sports. In *Torque* books, anything can happen. Are you ready?

This edition first published in 2027 by Bellwether Media, Inc.

For information regarding permission, write to Bellwether Media, Inc., Attention: Permissions Department, 3500 American Blvd W, Suite 150, Bloomington, MN 55431.

Library of Congress Cataloging-in-Publication Data is available at www.loc.gov or upon request from the publisher.

ISBN: 9798898801144 (hardcover)
ISBN: 9798898802738 (paperback)
ISBN: 9798898802387 (ebook)

Editor: Suzane Nyguen Designer: Josh Brink

Printed in the United States of America, North Mankato, MN.

TABLE OF CONTENTS

THE COMPETITORS

Freshwater **habitats** house fish of all shapes and sizes. Lampreys are an **invasive species** in many of them. These fish often feed on the blood of other animals.

Catfish often share waters with lampreys. Catfish open their mouths wide to eat any food near them. They easily sense **prey** and enemies in dark, muddy waters. Which freshwater **predator** is tougher?

Lampreys are eellike boneless fish. They can grow up to 3.3 feet (1 meter) long. Their smooth, narrow bodies are made of **cartilage**. Their jawless mouths have multiple rows of teeth.

Lampreys are found in **temperate** waters worldwide. They live in both salt water and fresh water. The fish prefer coastal areas, lakes, and rivers.

ANCIENT FISH

Lampreys existed before dinosaurs. Their history dates back around 450 million years.

SEA LAMPREY PROFILE

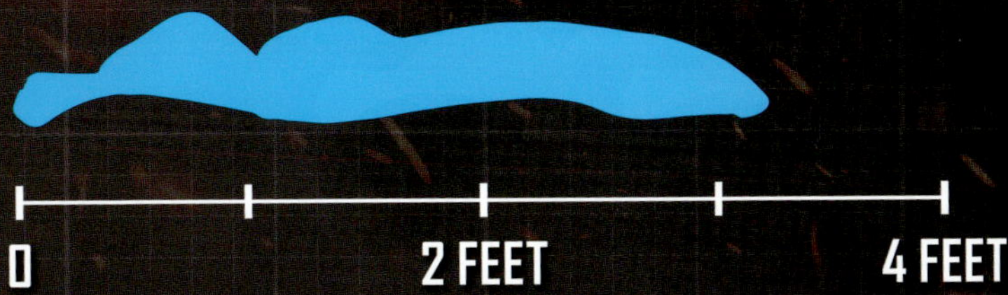

LENGTH

UP TO 3.3 FEET
(1 METER)

WEIGHT

UP TO 5 POUNDS
(2.3 KILOGRAMS)

HABITATS

COASTAL AREAS LAKES RIVERS

SEA LAMPREY RANGE

CHANNEL CATFISH PROFILE

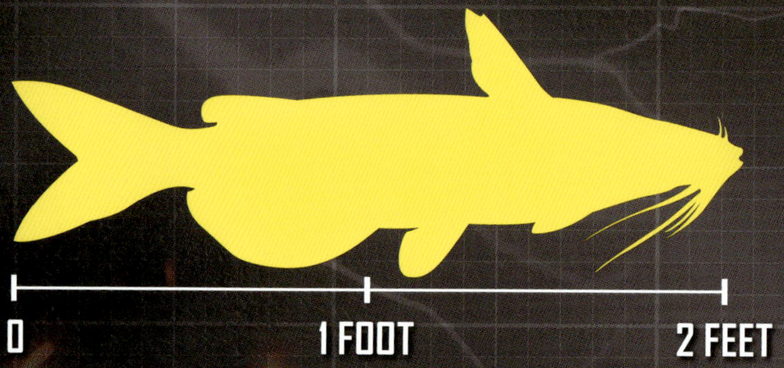

LENGTH

MORE THAN 2 FEET
(0.6 METERS)

WEIGHT

UP TO 4 POUNDS
(1.8 KILOGRAMS)

HABITATS

RIVERS STREAMS LAKES PONDS

CHANNEL CATFISH RANGE

Catfish are common freshwater fish. The largest grow more than 15 feet (4.6 meters) long. Their long, thick bodies have spiky fins and forked tails. Their flat heads have parts called **barbels**.

There are around 3,000 catfish **species**. Most live in fresh water. They prefer the muddy bottoms of rivers and streams.

THE LARGEST CATFISH

Wels catfish are one of the largest catfish. They can weigh up to 660 pounds (300 kilograms)!

SECRET WEAPONS

Lampreys have disclike mouths. This lets them stick to prey easily. The fish can open their mouths wider than their bodies! Their teeth help them dig into prey.

Catfish barbels are covered in thousands of taste buds. The fish use these to smell and feel their surroundings. They can find food without sight along dark river bottoms.

Lampreys have sharp tongues. These are lined with hornlike teeth. They use their tongues to cut holes in prey's skin. This makes for easy feeding!

INSIDE A LAMPREY'S MOUTH

ROWS OF TEETH

UP TO
7

MOUTH SIZE COMPARISON

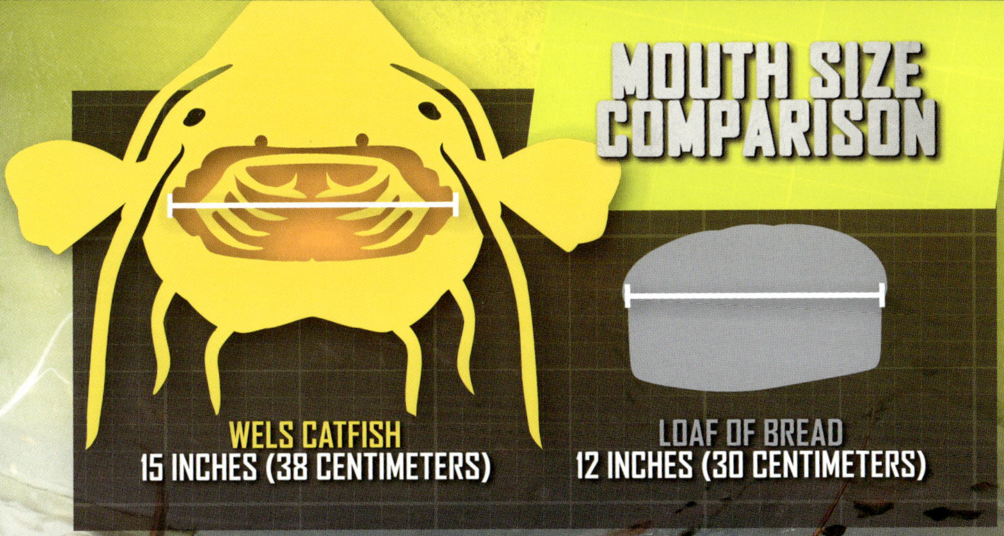

Catfish have large, wide mouths. They use these like a vacuum to suck in food. Their mouths also have tiny, backward-facing teeth. These help them hold on to slippery prey.

SECRET WEAPONS

LAMPREY

DISCLIKE MOUTH

SHARP TONGUE

SPECIAL SALIVA

Lampreys have special **saliva**. It has **chemicals** that keep prey's blood flowing. This helps lampreys eat for long periods. Some lampreys feed on one fish for weeks without stopping!

SECRET WEAPONS

CATFISH

BARBELS

LARGE MOUTH

SHARP FINS

Catfish have sharp fins. These hurt predators who try to attack them. They make catfish hard to swallow. Many species have fins that give off **venom**.

ATTACK MOVES

Most lampreys are **parasites**. They prefer large, slow-moving **hosts** such as trout and salmon. Some even feed on whales. They often attach to the sides of prey.

Most catfish are **opportunistic** eaters. They eat whatever they can find on river bottoms. Their diet includes crayfish, minnows, and snails. Some also suck up plants.

ELECTRIC CATFISH

Some catfish species can make electricity. They give painful shocks to prey and enemies.

POUNDS OF FISH

Lampreys eat a lot. One lamprey can eat up to 40 pounds (18 kilograms) of fish a year.

Lampreys tear into prey tongue-first after attaching to it. Then they feast on the prey's blood and skin. Freshwater hosts often become weakened from the blood loss. Many do not survive.

Catfish **ambush** their prey. They hide in holes or logs until prey swims by. Then they burst forward to suck it in! They often swallow prey whole.

READY, FIGHT!

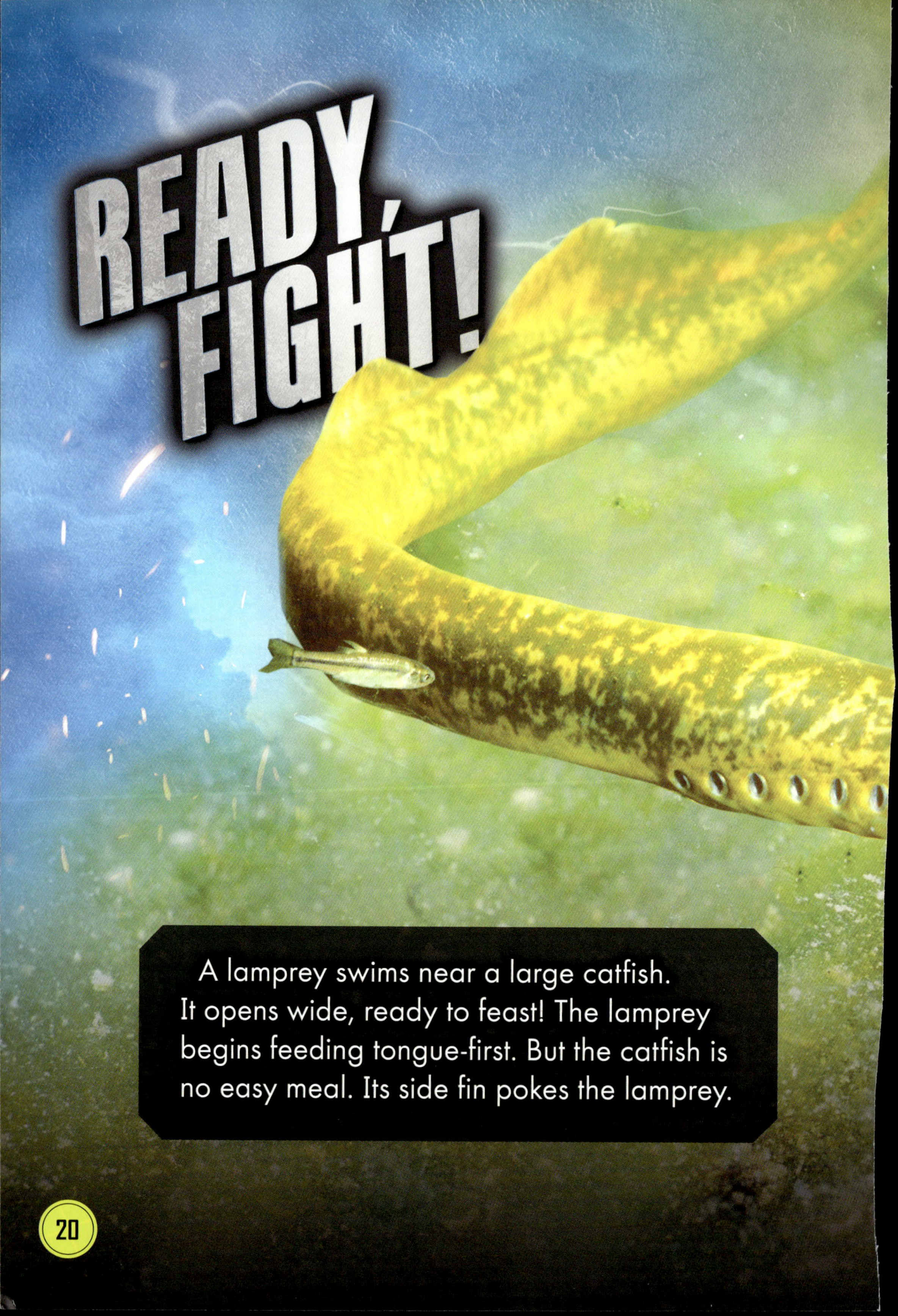

A lamprey swims near a large catfish. It opens wide, ready to feast! The lamprey begins feeding tongue-first. But the catfish is no easy meal. Its side fin pokes the lamprey.

The hurt lamprey tries to escape. The catfish finds it using its barbels. It sucks in the lamprey. The lamprey frees itself and swims away. The catfish has won the battle today!

GLOSSARY

ambush—to carry out a surprise attack

barbels—whisker-like body parts used to taste, smell, and feel

cartilage—stretchy tissue that makes up most of a lamprey's body

chemicals—materials that can cause a change in other materials

habitats—the homes or areas where animals prefer to live

hosts—animals that parasites live on or inside to feed off of

invasive species—a species that is not originally from a region and causes harm to its new environment

opportunistic—taking advantage of a situation

parasites—animals that feed off the blood and body fluids of other animals

predator—an animal that hunts other animals for food

prey—animals that are hunted by other animals for food

saliva—a watery fluid in the mouth that breaks down food

species—kinds of animals

temperate—related to ocean waters that have warm summers and cool winters

venom—a kind of poison used to hurt or paralyze enemies

TO LEARN MORE

AT THE LIBRARY

Becker, Trudy. *Sea Lampreys*. Mendota Heights, Minn.: Apex Editions, 2025.

Mattern, Joanne. *Mekong Giant Catfish*. Minneapolis, Minn.: Bellwether Media, 2024.

Terp, Gail. *Piraiba Catfish*. Mankato, Minn.: Black Rabbit Books, 2025.

ON THE WEB

FACTSURFER

Factsurfer.com gives you a safe, fun way to find more information.

1. Go to www.factsurfer.com.
2. Enter "lamprey vs. catfish" into the search box and click 🔍.
3. Select your book cover to see a list of related content.

INDEX

The images in this book are reproduced through the courtesy of: ИРИНА ОРЛОВА, front cover (lamprey); mathefoto, front cover (catfish); imageBROKER/ H. Frei/ Alamy Stock Photo, pp. 2 (catfish), 3 (catfish), 20 (catfish), 21 (catfish), 22 (catfish), 23 (catfish), 24 (catfish); Animals Animals/ SuperStock, pp. 2 (lamprey), 3 (lamprey), 20 (lamprey), 21 (lamprey), 22 (lamprey), 23 (lamprey), 24 (lamprey); Manuel E. Garci, p. 4; S Widodo, p. 5; Nick Hawkins/ Nature Picture Library, pp. 6-7; Aleron Val, pp. 8-9; Theresa Grace, p. 10; Colorshadow, p. 11; liveslow, p. 12; BongkarnC, p. 13; Gena Melendrez, p. 14 (disclike mouth); GDM photo and video, p. 14 (sharp tongue); annedehaas, p. 14 (special saliva); Great Lakes Fishery Commission, p. 14 (lamprey); 文普 王, p. 15 (barbels); robru, p. 15 (large mouth); Phil Lowe, p. 15 (sharp fins); Vladimir Wrangel, p. 15 (catfish); Jacana/ Science Source, p. 16; Rostislav, p. 17; Natural History Collection/ Alamy Stock Photo, p. 18; Alexander Iwan, p. 19.